THE TACKLING DIFFICULT CONVERSATIONS POCKETBOOK

By Peter English

Drawings by Phil Hailstone

"This book tells you everything you need to know to handle difficult conversations. It doesn't flinch from giving tough advice. ⬚⬚⬚⬚⬚⬚⬚⬚⬚ ⬚⬚⬚⬚⬚⬚⬚ wholeheartedly, and will use it as a resource for my coaching clients."
David Megginson, Professor Emeritu⬚
Sheffield Business School, Sheffield

Published by:
Management Pocketbooks Ltd
Laurel House, Station Approach, Alresford, Hants SO24 9JH, U.K.
Tel: +44 (0)1962 735573   Fax: +44 (0)1962 733637
Email: sales@pocketbook.co.uk
Website: www.pocketbook.co.uk

© Peter English 2009

This edition published 2009. Reprinted 2012, 2013.
ISBN 978 1 906610 04 3

E-book ISBN: 978 1 908284 14 3

British Library Cataloguing-in-Publication Data – A catalogue record for this book is available from the British Library.

Design, typesetting and graphics by **efex ltd**. Printed in U.K.

CONTENTS

HOW TO GET THE MOST FROM THIS BOOK

This book will show you how to prepare, and conduct, the kind of conversations that many people find challenging, for example:

- Asking someone to change their behaviour
- Saying 'no'
- Giving someone disappointing news
- Dealing with strong emotions
- Giving constructive criticism
- Responding in a professional manner when you are criticised

The book provides examples of how to apply these techniques in the workplace. The approaches will work equally well in social situations.

HOW TO GET THE MOST FROM THIS BOOK

This book is full of advice based on solid, real-life experience, combined with insights from business and social psychology. It will enable you to:

- Understand and deal with the uncomfortable feelings that can arise when you are facing a difficult conversation

- Prepare thoroughly for the conversation, so that you maximise the chances of a constructive outcome

- Deal confidently with the various kinds of difficult conversation that you are likely to face

 You will probably find the book most helpful if you read the early chapters on 'The Right Mindset' and 'Preparing for a Difficult Conversation', which give you the background, before looking at the later chapters, which cover a range of techniques you can use during a conversation.

6

THE RIGHT MINDSET

WHY WE AVOID DIFFICULT CONVERSATIONS

This chapter will help you understand why you may feel uncomfortable when faced with a difficult conversation, and how to respond to these feelings. **The key message of the chapter is that uncomfortable feelings are normal, but they shouldn't prevent you from having the conversation.**

We will look at:

- Comfort zones and stretch zones

- Why it is important to avoid 'toxic stamps'

- How to replace your 'head tapes' so that the need to be liked by other people does not dictate your actions

FEELING THE FEAR & DOING IT ANYWAY

If you find yourself in a situation where you dread saying what is needed, and are tempted to run away rather than confront the issue, it is important to remember that:

- As we go through life, **we are constantly confronted with challenges,** whether making a presentation for the first time, negotiating a particularly difficult deal or embarking on a new career

- **Meeting these challenges is what makes for a successful and fulfilling life.** It is how we grow and how we learn. Some conversations feel scary and difficult, but ultimately it is hard to have a satisfying life if we constantly shy away from challenges

COMFORT ZONES & STRETCH ZONES

One way of looking at your life is in terms of your comfort zone and your stretch zone.

You are in your comfort zone when you spend your time doing things that are easy, and that have predictable outcomes.

You start to move into your stretch zone when you take on something new, challenging or unpredictable.

Comfort Zone
Predictable
Safe Comfortable

Stretch Zone
Challenging - Exciting - Developmental

THE RIGHT MINDSET

LEAVING YOUR COMFORT ZONE

Tackling a difficult conversation is probably an example of something that takes you out of your comfort zone. If you try, however, to arrange your life so that you never leave your comfort zone you will become:

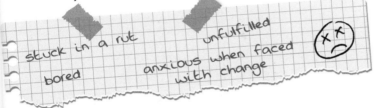

stuck in a rut

bored

unfulfilled

anxious when faced with change

The answer is not to spend your whole life in your stretch zone (unless you thrive on constant challenge and excitement) but to spend time in both zones.

It does get easier with practice – as you stretch yourself, you grow in confidence, thus expanding what comes naturally and creating a newer, bigger comfort zone.

THE RIGHT MINDSET

DON'T COLLECT STAMPS

Some years ago, in the UK, retailers used to give customers Green Shield Stamps when they made a purchase. The stamps would be stuck in a book, and full books could be exchanged for a free item – a bit like supermarket loyalty card points.

Each of us has a stamp book inside us! However, **the stamps are toxic and are better avoided.** Whenever you shy away from confronting something you are unhappy about, it is as if you take a stamp and stick it inside yourself – a feeling of resentment or misery. Once your book is full you have no room for new stamps, and the next time one comes your way you explode at the person who is in front of you – you cash in the whole book.

Top Tip

Collecting toxic stamps makes you miserable and depressed. In organisations, too much stamp collecting leads to resentment and a bad atmosphere. So, try not to take on stamps – if you aren't happy with how someone is treating you, confront them about it quickly.

THE RIGHT MINDSET

'BUT I WANT PEOPLE TO LIKE ME!'

Wanting to be liked by other people is natural, but if you let your need to be liked dominate the way that you behave you will cause problems for yourself. For example, many managers find that the hardest aspect of their job is not learning how to delegate or how to handle competing priorities – it is overcoming their need to be liked by their staff. If you let your need to be liked by others take over, you will find yourself:

- Saying 'yes' to people when you want to say 'no'
- Doing things that you don't really want to do, just to keep the other person happy
- Avoiding making decisions that you fear will be unpopular
- Becoming resentful

Top Tip — If you spend your time trying to get people to like you, they may end up seeing you as a doormat. If your aim is for them to respect you, they may end up liking you anyway.

13

THE RIGHT MINDSET

REPLACE SOME OF YOUR HEAD TAPES

Head tapes are (often unconsciously held) beliefs that we have about how we should behave. They are usually messages that we have picked up in childhood from our parents and teachers. Here are some examples of things that we say to ourselves:

'It's terrible if someone is angry with me'

'Putting myself first makes me a bad person'

'I must never disappoint anyone'

'Trying to get what you want is selfish'

A good exercise, when you are feeling uncomfortable about your relationship with another person, is to identify which head tape is playing. Once you have identified the head tape you can replace it with another, more helpful, tape.

THE RIGHT MINDSET

REPLACE SOME OF YOUR HEAD TAPES

Here are some examples of unhelpful and helpful head tapes.

Old unhelpful head tape	New helpful head tape
'It's terrible if someone is angry with me'	'I might be uncomfortable but it's not the end of the world. Their anger is their problem'
'Putting myself first makes me a bad person'	'I need to look after myself so I'm able to look after others'
'I must never disappoint anyone'	'People are going to be disappointed sometimes. It's unavoidable'
'Trying to get what you want is selfish'	'It's OK to meet my needs, so long as I don't trample on other people'

THE RIGHT MINDSET

USE THE RIGHT SUBPERSONALITY

You may find yourself thinking that you have just one personality. Perhaps you say to yourself, *'I am a kind person'* or, *'I am a timid person'*. The reality is, however, that we all have lots of different modes of feeling or behaving, depending on the situation. Think of yourself as having several **subpersonalities.** For example:

- A wise old person
- A powerful warrior
- A playful child
- A calm, mature adult

When you go into a new situation, think about which of your subpersonalities you want to take the lead.

The **key message from this chapter** is that if you avoid tackling the difficult conversation, there will be a cost to yourself and others. Often, getting into the right mindset is more than half the battle.

PREPARING FOR A
DIFFICULT CONVERSATION

THE IMPORTANCE OF PREPARATION

There are some conversations where you can anticipate resistance from the other person, for example when you are:

- Giving a team member feedback that their performance needs to improve
- Telling someone that you are unhappy with their behaviour
- Persuading someone to take on extra responsibility

Many people spend a lot of time worrying about the resistance they are likely to encounter, but fail to undertake some constructive preparation for the conversation. This chapter outlines how to prepare by:

- Defining your objective
- Deciding what sort of 'yes' you want
- Considering how to manage the emotional bank account
- Thinking about the style and tone you want to adopt

PREPARING FOR A DIFFICULT CONVERSATION

HAVE A CLEAR OBJECTIVE

For conversations you can anticipate and plan for, it is very important to decide on your objective before the conversation. Many people go into a conversation with only a vague sense of what they hope to achieve, then wonder why it didn't go the way they had hoped. Your objectives might include:

- Getting the other person to agree to a specific course of action
- Letting the other person know how you feel

Don't expect an apology

In my experience, expecting an apology from the other person might be ambitious, even if you firmly believe that they are in the wrong. Rather than aiming for an apology, your objective should be to let them know how you feel about their behaviour, and the impact it had on you.

PREPARING FOR A DIFFICULT CONVERSATION

WHAT SORT OF 'YES' DO YOU WANT?

If you want the other person to say 'yes' or agree to something, it is worth thinking through the kind of 'yes' that you want. A 'yes' can mean anything from wholehearted agreement and commitment, to determined resistance. The person might be saying:

- *'I completely agree. You have my wholehearted support'*
  or
- *'You seem to think this is a good idea and I want the conversation to be over so I'll just say yes'*
  or
- *'It won't look good if I say no, so I'll appear to go along with this, but there's no way I'm going to do what you want'*

You don't always need a committed 'yes' from the other person. For example, when getting your money refunded in a shop you don't need the salesperson to feel delighted about it.

PREPARING FOR A DIFFICULT CONVERSATION

THE EMOTIONAL BANK ACCOUNT

Stephen Covey's book, *The Seven Habits of Highly Effective People,* describes how relationships can be viewed as containing an **invisible emotional bank account.** If the relationship is a good one where you like and respect one another, and share some common aims, you can say that there is a lot of credit in the account.

The emotional bank account works on the **principle of reciprocity.** Reciprocity is a powerful force in many cultures – it is the feeling of indebtedness we experience when someone has done us a favour. So, if the neighbours invite you round for dinner or drinks, you feel obliged to invite them to your house at some point.

If your emotional bank account remains in credit, the relationship will feel relatively easy and pleasant. But **if the account becomes overdrawn** you will start to experience it as a difficult relationship, and there is a danger that you will see each other as enemies.

THE EMOTIONAL BANK ACCOUNT

INVESTMENTS & WITHDRAWALS

We increase our credit in the emotional bank account by making investments or deposits – ie, doing things that make the other person like us more. Examples of these are:

- Helping the other person
- Paying them a (genuine) compliment
- Showing interest in what they are saying

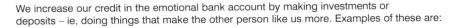

We can also make withdrawals from the account:

- Saying 'no' to the other person when they ask for help
- Asking the other person to change their behaviour

Some withdrawals should always be avoided (eg, criticising someone harshly in front of other people), but others are, on occasion, inevitable (eg, saying you are too busy to help).

PREPARING FOR A DIFFICULT CONVERSATION

THE EMOTIONAL BANK ACCOUNT
AS A FACTOR IN DIFFICULT CONVERSATIONS

We need to bear in mind the emotional bank account when contemplating a difficult conversation because **the conversation itself will *usually* count as a withdrawal** – the account will take a dip during and after the encounter.

Occasionally, however, the difficult conversation may count as investment – this can be the case where you both talk about your feelings and understand each other better as a result. This can strengthen the relationship.

It is really important to keep **consciously and deliberately investing in your relationships** with anyone you need to get on well with, whether a partner, a colleague, a neighbour or a boss. If you have a lot of credit in the emotional bank account, you are less likely to become overdrawn as a result of a difficult conversation. If you have neglected to invest in the relationship, however, your account can easily slip into the red when you are talking about a difficult issue.

PREPARING FOR A DIFFICULT CONVERSATION

STYLE & TONE

Think in advance about the style and tone that you want to adopt in the conversation. One way of assessing the different styles you might use is to consider the ego state model, which was first described by Eric Berne in the 1960s.

According to the model, when we are relating to another person, we can behave in three main ways. We can act like:

A parent   An adult   A child

Each of these ways of behaving is called an ego state.

STYLE & TONE

EGO STATES & DIFFICULT CONVERSATIONS

Difficult conversations can produce quite marked demonstrations of parent or child behaviour.

Examples

- If a person becomes upset or loses their temper they are probably acting from a **child** state

- If one party is trying to tell the other person off, they are probably in a **parent** state

Generally, parent or child states are unhelpful when tackling difficult conversations. The most constructive approach is for both parties to use the **adult** state.

STYLE & TONE

PARENT EGO STATE

In the parent state we can adopt either a nurturing or a controlling style. When we are in the **nurturing parent** state we are concerned with the other person's feelings – we might want them to feel comfortable, encouraged, soothed. In the **controlling parent** state our focus is getting the person to undertake a task properly.

Every day you can see people, especially managers, using the nurturing or controlling style in the workplace.

For example, you might notice that a colleague is looking stressed, and say to them, *'Are you OK? You look a bit tired. Would you like a coffee?'* This is **nurturing parent** behaviour.

An example of **controlling parent** behaviour would be saying to a new member of staff, *'Here's how we do this piece of work. When you're doing it, be careful not to make this particular mistake, and come and show me what you've done when you've finished.'*

PREPARING FOR A DIFFICULT CONVERSATION

STYLE & TONE
ADULT EGO STATE

The adult ego state involves acting in a logical, matter of fact way. It is often appropriate when trying to solve a problem. The adult state is also the part of us that is self-aware, and manages our own behaviour – choosing how to act in a particular situation.

An example of the **logical problem solver adult** would be talking to your manager about a problem within the department, and putting your heads together to try to think of a solution. Note that two people can have an adult to adult conversation irrespective of their relative positions in the organisation's hierarchy.

An example of the **self-aware adult** might be when you are going to an event and you intend to use the opportunity to network with a particular group of people. If you were in adult mode, you would plan your approach in advance, then be quite deliberate and focused about who you talked to when you were there.

STYLE & TONE
CHILD EGO STATE

In the child state we can act like a natural child or an adapted child. **Natural child** behaviour is when we express ourselves in an uninhibited way – having fun, laughing, complaining, having a tantrum.

When a person is in the **adapted child** state they are primarily concerned with relating to rules and an authority figure. A person exhibiting adapted child behaviour may behave in a compliant way (wanting to obey the rules and please the authority figure) or a rebellious way (breaking the rules and disobeying the authority figure).

PREPARING FOR A DIFFICULT CONVERSATION

STYLE & TONE

EGO STATE INTERACTIONS

When you are talking to another person, your ego state will be interacting with their ego state. For example:

- If you are both primarily concerned with sorting out a problem, you might both be in the **adult** state

- If the other person is coming to you for advice and support, they might be in the **adapted child** state and wanting you to act like a parent

- If you are arguing with someone about their behaviour, and you each want to have the last word, you might find that you have both moved into the **parent** state and are trying to tell one another off

- If you are having fun and laughing together you will probably both be in the **natural child** state

STYLE & TONE

EGO STATE INTERACTIONS

It is important to recognise that when another person is in a particular ego state **it can cause you to feel that you should act in the corresponding way.** For example, if you are a manager with a team of people who are reluctant to take responsibility (ie, they are acting from a child state) you might find yourself feeling, and behaving, like an exasperated parent.

On the other hand, if you are someone who likes to be in control of situations, and to have the last word in any encounter, you may find that the people around you start to behave in more childish ways.

Often these kinds of interactions are positive – your partner is upset and in a child state, so you respond with nurturing parent behaviour. We can, however, sometimes find ourselves being unwittingly set up to assume the parent or child role in a personal or professional relationship, even if we wouldn't consciously choose to do so.

STYLE & TONE

USING THE ADULT STATE

You stand the best chance of creating a constructive atmosphere and achieving a positive outcome if you use the adult ego state. This means:

- **Being aware of your own feelings and behaviour,** and consciously choosing what you say and how you say it

- **Focusing on solving the problem** rather than trying to win the argument or 'put the other person in their place'

Even if the other person is acting from a parent or child state, you can still use language which shows that you are in an adult state:

'I understand you're unhappy about this. I'd like to find a way of resolving the situation.'

'I'm sorry that you feel uncomfortable. How can we sort things out?'

STYLE & TONE
THE CONTROLLING PARENT TRAP

A big pitfall in a difficult conversation is one of the parties moving into controlling parent mode. This usually results in the other person responding like a rebellious adapted child, or themselves going into a controlling parent state, leading to a power struggle.

Examples of the controlling parent state in a difficult conversation are:

- Using phrases like *you should, you must, you ought to* or generalisations: *you always or you never*
- Talking over the other person, interrupting them
- Adopting a disapproving tone of voice

If you find that you are moving into parent mode, try to catch yourself quickly and move back into the adult state.

PREPARING FOR A DIFFICULT CONVERSATION

STYLE & TONE
THE ADAPTED CHILD TRAP

If you are feeling anxious before a difficult conversation, particularly if you view the other person as being more powerful than you, it is easy to fall into the adapted child trap. In this situation, it is often body language that gives the game away – a person in the adapted child state will sit like a child about to be told off by the headteacher.

The body language of the adapted child state includes:

- Sitting forward on the edge of your seat
- Looking up at the other person
- Inconsistent eye contact
- Feet together
- Hands clenched in the lap

33

PREPARING FOR A DIFFICULT CONVERSATION

STYLE & TONE
THE NURTURING PARENT TRAP

The child's message
The person in the child role gives the unspoken message, *'If you criticise or confront me you are a bad person, because I am fragile'*. Sometimes the person genuinely believes that they are fragile, though on other occasions they are playing a manipulative game.

The parent's response
When faced with the hurt child behaviour, the other person feels two conflicting impulses: they want to address the issue, but they also feel they should act like a nurturing parent and soothe the other person's hurt feelings.

In this situation it is important to keep yourself in the adult state and focus on calmly addressing the issue. Say something like, *'I'm sorry that you are feeling hurt. I would like us to resolve this issue so that neither of us feels uncomfortable'*.

CREATING THE RIGHT ATMOSPHERE

WHY ATMOSPHERE IS IMPORTANT

The outcome of some difficult conversations is decided in the first few moments of the interaction. If you get these right, you have a greater chance of a successful encounter. This chapter takes you through the different aspects you need to consider when creating the right atmosphere, namely:

- Acknowledging, and adapting, your habitual approach to conflict

- Thinking through your opening lines

- Taking into account some practical considerations

- The golden rule of influencing

HABITUAL APPROACHES TO CONFLICT

Taking some time to create the right atmosphere at the start of the conversation can make a big difference as to whether it goes well or turns into an unpleasant argument. The first thing to think about is whether you are naturally a competer or an accommodator.

Most people have an habitual way of approaching difficult conversations – I call this our **default setting.** Our default setting is a combination of:

- How much we want to win the conversation, and get a result that we are happy with. This is our **competing** inclination

- The extent to which we want the other person to feel good during and after the conversation – how concerned we are that they get their needs met. This is our **accommodating** inclination

HABITUAL APPROACHES TO CONFLICT
FIVE APPROACHES TO HANDLING CONFLICT

In 1974 Kenneth W Thomas and Ralph H Kilmann created a model which combines our tendency to compete and our tendency to accommodate, giving five approaches to handling conflict.

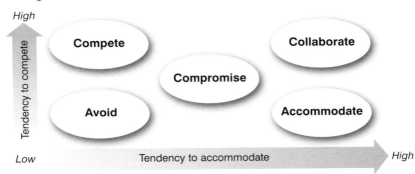

CREATING THE RIGHT ATMOSPHERE

HABITUAL APPROACHES TO CONFLICT

UNDERSTANDING THE FIVE STYLES

Each of us has a preference for one or two of the five styles.

Competers	Natural inclination in a difficult conversation is to win. Less concerned about the other person's feelings.
Accommodators	Want to maintain the relationship on good terms. They don't mind if they don't get their needs met so long as the other person is happy.
Compromisers	Prefer to 'do a deal' that both can live with rather than spend ages thrashing out an agreement that fully meets their needs.
Avoiders	Strong preference to avoid the difficult conversation. The issue doesn't get resolved: they aren't happy and neither is the other person.
Collaborators	Want a result that meets their needs and those of the other person. Prepared to invest the time and energy in fully resolving the issue.

CREATING THE RIGHT ATMOSPHERE

HABITUAL APPROACHES TO CONFLICT

WHICH STYLE TO USE?

Style	When to use
Compete	When you want to get your needs met, and you are not concerned about maintaining a relationship, for example, when asking for a refund in a shop.
Accommodate	In situations where the relationship takes priority, with your immediate needs taking second place.
Compromise	When time is short and you need to agree a practical resolution that you can both live with.
Avoid	This means you don't have the difficult conversation at all! It can be appropriate in situations where things are likely to change anyway (eg, if one of you will be leaving the organisation shortly).
Collaborate	When you will be having an ongoing relationship with the other person and you both need to feel that your needs are being met.

CREATING THE RIGHT ATMOSPHERE

HABITUAL APPROACHES TO CONFLICT

HOW TO BEGIN THE CONVERSATION

Once you have decided which style you want to use, you can create the appropriate atmosphere at the start of the conversation.

Style	Examples of what to say
Compete	*'I'm really unhappy about this faulty product and I want a refund.'*
Accommodate	*I know that you are concerned about this situation and I want us to find a resolution that you are happy with.'*
Compromise	*'I'd like us to sort this out and strike a deal that we can both live with.'*
Avoid	*Either you don't have the conversation, or you say, 'I think it would be better if we didn't discuss this' when the other person raises the issue.*
Collaborate	*'I'm really keen that we take the time to resolve this issue fully and that we both walk away happy with the outcome.'*

THE GOLDEN RULE OF INFLUENCING

When you are trying to get a positive outcome from a difficult conversation, it's worth remembering that the golden rule of influencing is:

> CREATE RAPPORT BEFORE YOU TRY TO PERSUADE

This means taking some time at the start of the conversation to create an atmosphere whereby, even though you and the other person might have different views, you are approaching the issue as a shared problem to be solved rather than a fight that you each want to win.

There are two powerful techniques for creating rapport:

1. **The emotional bank account** (described in the previous chapter).

2. **Mirroring.**

HABITUAL APPROACHES TO CONFLICT

HOW TO BEGIN THE CONVERSATION

Once you have decided which style you want to use, you can create the appropriate atmosphere at the start of the conversation.

Style	Examples of what to say
Compete	*'I'm really unhappy about this faulty product and I want a refund.'*
Accommodate	*'I know that you are concerned about this situation and I want us to find a resolution that you are happy with.'*
Compromise	*'I'd like us to sort this out and strike a deal that we can both live with.'*
Avoid	*Either you don't have the conversation, or you say, 'I think it would be better if we didn't discuss this' when the other person raises the issue.*
Collaborate	*'I'm really keen that we take the time to resolve this issue fully and that we both walk away happy with the outcome.'*

CREATING THE RIGHT ATMOSPHERE

YOUR OPENING LINES

When deciding how to start the conversation you need to think about whether you want to downplay or emphasise the importance of what you are going to talk about. You might want to **downplay the importance** if you are concerned that the person might have an overly strong emotional reaction to what you are about to say. If this is the case, you might say something like:

'I want to have a chat with you about something that is bothering me a little. It's not a big deal, but I do want to talk about it.'

You may want to **emphasise the importance** if you suspect that the other person may not realise the significance of what you want to talk about, or that they might try to be dismissive. You could say:

'I want to talk to you about something that I am concerned about. I think that we both might find this a difficult conversation, and I want us both to be as constructive as possible during it.'

CREATING THE RIGHT ATMOSPHERE

PRACTICAL CONSIDERATIONS

The venue
Generally, somewhere that you won't be overheard is best, and if you are working in a glass-walled office you might want to draw the blinds. If you are in a work setting, think about whether you need to book a meeting room so that you are both on neutral territory.

Giving the other person notice
Sometimes it is helpful to give the other person some notice that you want to talk to them: *'I'd like to talk to you about x, could we fix a time tomorrow?'* This gives them a chance to think about what they want to say. If you don't give the other person notice, ask them, *'Is this a convenient time?'* when you approach them. If they say that it isn't, then arrange a time that is convenient for both of you.

Timing
Don't try and have the conversation when either party is feeling particularly stressed.

THE GOLDEN RULE OF INFLUENCING

When you are trying to get a positive outcome from a difficult conversation, it's worth remembering that the golden rule of influencing is:

> CREATE RAPPORT BEFORE YOU TRY TO PERSUADE

This means taking some time at the start of the conversation to create an atmosphere whereby, even though you and the other person might have different views, you are approaching the issue as a shared problem to be solved rather than a fight that you each want to win.

There are two powerful techniques for creating rapport:

1. **The emotional bank account** (described in the previous chapter).

2. **Mirroring.**

CREATING THE RIGHT ATMOSPHERE

MIRRORING

WHAT IS MIRRORING?

Have you ever noticed how if one person in a train carriage coughs, other people will cough as well?

Mirroring means **copying the other person's body language and speech patterns.** It is something that human beings do every day – in any social setting you will see people unconsciously mirroring their friends in the way that they sit, and in their levels of animation.

We start mirroring early in life – if you watch a mother interacting with a young baby you will notice an enormous amount of subtle mirroring going on as each copies the other's facial expressions.

Mirroring is a useful technique at the start of a difficult conversation because it creates the sense that **we are on the same wavelength.** Done well, it generates a feeling of rapport, which can be vital in ensuring that a difficult conversation goes smoothly.

CREATING THE RIGHT ATMOSPHERE

MIRRORING
HOW DO I DO IT?

To mirror someone in a powerful but unobtrusive way, focus on two things:

- The other person's posture
- Their level of animation

Mirroring their posture means noticing whether or not they are standing or sitting in a relaxed manner or a more formal pose. It also means being aware of whether the person is leaning forward (to engage you) or leaning back (to create more personal space).

Top Tip
If the other person is leaning back in their chair, in a fairly relaxed pose, you should adopt a similar position. Avoid the (natural) temptation to lean forward, as this may make them want to move further away.

CREATING THE RIGHT ATMOSPHERE

MIRRORING
MATCHING LEVELS OF ANIMATION

Mirroring the other person's level of animation involves picking up on whether they are expressing themselves in a relatively quiet, composed and reserved manner or whether they are using lots of gestures, facial expressions and movements to communicate their point. You then try to match their level of animation.

Example
Imagine that you are naturally an expressive and animated person and that you are likely to behave this way in a difficult conversation. If you are dealing with someone who has a more quiet and reserved style there will be a sense that you are not on the same wavelength – unless you mirror them.

So, in this situation, you would need to **deliberately damp down your naturally animated style** and behave in a quieter, less expressive fashion.

MIRRORING

TWO APPROACHES

There are two ways of approaching mirroring: empathy and observation.

1. Empathise
Using the empathic approach to mirroring means listening intently to the other person and using your imagination to understand how they are feeling, and how the situation looks from their perspective.

Empathising with the other person will often result in you mirroring them naturally.

CREATING THE RIGHT ATMOSPHERE

MIRRORING

TWO APPROACHES

2. Observe

This approach involves focusing carefully on the other person's body language, facial expressions and gestures. Gently begin to copy them, but in a low-key way.

For example, if the other person is using their hands in an animated way, you could move your hands in your lap – this is called 'echoing'. Or if they are tapping their fingers, you could tap your feet.

CREATING THE RIGHT ATMOSPHERE

MIRRORING

WHAT IF THE OTHER PERSON IS ANGRY?

Case Study A

Some years ago I was unhappy with the quality of some flooring that a department store had supplied and fitted. After a few weeks of trying to resolve the problem over the telephone I went to the shop and asked to speak to the manager. By this time I was quite angry. When the manager appeared, I gave vent to my feelings – speaking quickly, staccato gestures, frowning expression. The manager responded by mirroring me! He nodded vigorously and frowned as I was talking, but in a way that indicated concern rather than anger.

After a few moments I noticed that I was feeling less angry: I had a sense that the manager was on my wavelength, and sharing my concern at the poor service. It was only later that I realised the manager had calmed me down by mirroring me.

Important: don't try to use mirroring if the other person is acting in an aggressive or threatening manner.

INCREASING YOUR IMPACT

HOW DO YOU MAKE AN IMPACT?

We instinctively tend to listen to people who appear powerful and authoritative. Some people have a naturally commanding air, but there are specific things that we can all do (or avoid doing) in order to have more impact in a conversation. This chapter describes a range of techniques which will:

- Encourage people to take you seriously

- Help you to manage your body language

- Allow you to take control of the conversation

- Enable you to be more successful at influencing different kinds of people

AVOIDING THE CHILD POSE

Remember the adapted child trap described in chapter two? In terms of capturing the other person's attention, adopting the child pose conveys the message, through your body language, that:
'I am nervous and unsure of myself. I will let you take the lead'.
If the other person is a bully, they may read this body language as an invitation to ignore what you have to say.

A more powerful alternative to the adapted child pose is to **push yourself back in your chair and cross your legs.** This prevents you from leaning forward and conveys a sense that you are listening to the other person, but not hanging on their every word. You can fold your hands in your lap in this posture, without appearing submissive.

CONTROL YOUR GIVEAWAYS

Giveaways are the physical ways in which anxiety can leak out when we are talking to another person. Examples are:

- Twisting hands

- Touching your own face or hair

- Fiddling with a pen

Like the child pose, giveaways can make it easy for the other person to ignore what you are saying, because **they broadcast a message that you are not feeling confident or powerful,** and you are therefore unlikely to persist if the other person tries to avoid the conversation or ignore you.

54

USE QUESTIONS DELIBERATELY

HIGH RISING INTONATION

A common pitfall, when faced with someone who we find intimidating, is to turn everything we say into a question. This is conveyed by **raising the intonation at the end of the sentence.**

For example, a new manager who is keen to get on well with an intimidating team member might say, *'Could you do this typing for me?'* (with the voice rising on the word 'me', turning the request into a question that invites a refusal if the team member doesn't want to do the typing).

This inflection betrays a lack of conviction, and suggests to the other person that you are expecting a refusal. **Without the upward inflection on the 'me', the request would sound much more powerful,** as though you expect the other person to say 'yes'. In observing difficult conversations, I sometimes notice that one person sounds as though they are asking a favour or pleading with the other – this impression is often created by the questioning tone of the raised intonation on the last word – and it is not persuasive.

INCREASING YOUR IMPACT

USE QUESTIONS DELIBERATELY

TAKE CONTROL OF THE CONVERSATION

Although turning every statement into a question through raised voice intonation can convey weakness, **using questions deliberately can make it harder for someone to avoid engaging with you.** It is a common misconception that the person who has most power in a conversation is the one who does most of the talking. In fact, you can exert more power by using questions to probe the other person's point of view, and make them justify their position – like a barrister cross-examining a witness in court.

Imagine that one of your team is too laid back, and regularly misses deadlines. Instead of talking at them (which will probably result in their mentally switching off) you can use questions to exert pressure on them to discuss the subject. For example:

- *'Tell me about what happened with that last piece of work'*
- *'How did you view the deadline? Did you see it as flexible?'*
- *'How could we ensure that you meet deadlines in future?'*

COMMENT ON THEIR REACTION

If you feel that the other person is not listening to you, a powerful way of gaining their attention is to comment calmly on what they are doing. For example, you might say something like:

> *'I'm noticing that you are looking at your email while I'm talking and I feel that you're not listening to me.'*

If the other person does not respond, you can make your point more powerfully by talking about how their lack of reaction makes you feel:

> *'When you don't listen to me I feel angry. My view is that these are important things that we need to talk about, and it worries me that you don't seem willing to engage in the conversation.'*

It is important to express this in a neutral rather than accusatory tone of voice, otherwise the other person is likely to become defensive.

TAILOR YOUR LANGUAGE

In terms of motivation, people can be broadly divided into two types.

'Towards' types are motivated to move towards things that attract them. They become enthusiastic about things that appeal to them.

'Away Froms' are motivated by their desire to move away from things that they don't want – to prevent bad things from happening. They become anxious about things that concern them.

If you want to capture someone's attention, then use language that will appeal to their 'towards' or 'away from' orientation.

A **'Towards'** type needs to hear about positive outcomes and exciting opportunities. Use phrases like: *'Wouldn't it be great if...'*

An **'Away From'** will respond to you talking about risks and things to avoid. Use phrases like: *'We need to be careful about...'*

COPING WITH CRITICISM

HANDLING OUR OWN DEFENSIVE FEELINGS

This chapter covers ways of dealing with people who are criticising you. **The key message of the section is that being criticised often makes us feel defensive, but our feelings shouldn't dictate how we handle the conversation.** The chapter describes:

- The instinctive 'fight or flight' response, and how it affects us when we are criticised

- A four-step process to use when you feel yourself becoming defensive

- The three responses you can give to someone who is criticising you

THE FIGHT OR FLIGHT RESPONSE

The fight or flight response is one of our most powerful human instincts. Imagine yourself living 10,000 years ago in a hostile environment where fierce creatures would have regarded you as a potential meal. If you sensed a dangerous animal suddenly approaching, there wouldn't be time to carry out a thorough risk assessment of the situation. Instead, you would register the threat to your life, and various physiological processes would kick in to help you run away as fast as possible. For example, adrenalin would be released and your heart would beat faster to supply your muscles with blood. In other words you would experience the **flight** response.

If, however, the animal had you cornered and you had nowhere to run, the same physiological processes would help you respond ferociously to defend yourself, and you would experience a **fight** response.

COPING WITH CRITICISM

WHEN FIGHT OR FLIGHT ISN'T HELPFUL

Ten thousand years ago the fight or flight response was an important aid to survival. Now we only rarely need this powerful instinctive reaction. Unfortunately we can't just switch it off: there are times when it is triggered in ways that can be unproductive.

The fight or flight response is triggered by some kind of **threat.** Thousands of years ago the threat was to our physical safety. Nowadays the threats that make us defensive are more subtle, eg:

- When we fear we might lose something important to us
- If our self-image is challenged
- When our sense of self-worth comes under attack

These are **psychological** rather than physical threats, but they can still trigger a fight or flight reaction in us, and lead to defensive or unhelpful behaviour in the context of a difficult conversation.

FEATURES OF THE FLIGHT RESPONSE

Imagine that someone is criticising you harshly – really finding fault – and you are starting to feel under attack. In this context the threat is to your pride (it feels humiliating to be spoken to in this way) and to your self-esteem (you wonder if there may be some truth in their criticism). A fight or flight response in this situation is very common. A **flight** response is characterised by:

Fidgeting

Not making eye contact with the other person

Not saying much

Flushing

Speaking quietly or stuttering

Adopting a submissive pose – head down, shoulders hunched

If someone criticises you and you adopt a flight response you will come away from the situation feeling embarrassed, humiliated and conscious that you haven't handled the conversation well.

63

FEATURES OF THE FIGHT RESPONSE

In the same situation, where someone is criticising you, a **fight** response is characterised by:

Strong eye contact

Moving closer to the other person

Talking more loudly

More animation

Jabbing gestures (eg finger pointing)

Speaking over the other person

If your response to criticism is to adopt the fight response, it is likely that the conversation will become heated and that you risk damaging your relationship with the other person.

COPING WITH CRITICISM

CONTROLLING YOUR RESPONSE
STEP 1 : NOTICE WHEN IT IS HAPPENING

When you find yourself in a situation where you are responding angrily or defensively to criticism, the first step is to notice your feelings. This will help to prevent them from taking over. You say to yourself, *'I can feel myself getting angry, but that's OK, it's a normal human fight response. I don't have to express my anger.'*

For some of us, particularly if we are quite expressive people, catching our fight or flight response before acting on it can be quite a challenge. **The trick is to avoid responding too soon to the criticism.**

COPING WITH CRITICISM

CONTROLLING YOUR RESPONSE
STEP 2 : LISTEN

Listening to the other person does three things:

- It enables you to hear what they are unhappy about

- It allows them to express themselves without being interrupted

- It buys you time to notice, and control, your fight or flight response

CONTROLLING YOUR RESPONSE

STEP 3 : ASK QUESTIONS

Once you have heard the other person's criticism, the temptation is to reply, either by apologising and making excuses, or by arguing. Both of these approaches are likely to lead to a negative outcome. Instead of responding to the criticism, ask some questions. This enables you to:

- Find out more about what the person is unhappy about (was it just a one-off occasion, or has it been an ongoing problem for them?)

- Buy yourself more time to control your response

- Give them the message that you are prepared to have a mature, rational discussion about the issue

CONTROLLING YOUR RESPONSE
TIPS WHEN USING QUESTIONS

It is important when you ask your questions that you:

- Avoid using the questions to 'score points' eg, *'Are you seriously suggesting that....?'* Questions like this will be heard as challenges, and are more likely to result in both sides going into fight mode

- Resist the temptation to bombard the other person with questions designed to show that they are wrong, eg, *'What evidence do you have that I wasn't being careful? How do you know that I wasn't simply unlucky?'* This kind of cross-examination is likely to lead to an argument

- Maintain a neutral voice tone. If you sound defensive or aggressive, the other person is likely to hear this as a fight or flight response and react accordingly

COPING WITH CRITICISM

CONTROLLING YOUR RESPONSE
STEP **4** : RESPOND

Once you have noticed, and controlled, your fight or
flight response, listened to what the other person has
to say and asked questions to help you understand
their viewpoint, you are in a position to respond
to their criticism. Essentially, there are three
possible responses:

1 Accept the criticism.

2 Disagree with the criticism.

3 Ask for time.

CONTROLLING YOUR RESPONSE

OPTION **1**: ACCEPT THE CRITICISM

> *'I understand what you're saying, and you're right. I'm sorry,
> and here's how I'll do things differently next time.....'*

Although this can be a hard thing to say, you are likely to walk away from the
conversation pleased with how you handled it, and with the other person respecting
you for your maturity and honesty.

You will also have learned something from the other person's feedback.

CONTROLLING YOUR RESPONSE
OPTION **2** : DISAGREE WITH THE CRITICISM

> *'I think I have understood what you are saying, and I can see how the situation looks from your perspective. I don't see things the same way. Here's my view.....'*

This is likely to lead to the conversation continuing, and while it may not be particularly comfortable, it is more likely to be a constructive encounter than if you had simply responded emotionally (from the fight response) when the person first articulated their criticism.

As the conversation continues, you need to go into **problem solving mode** to see if there is a way that you can both get your needs met.

CONTROLLING YOUR RESPONSE
OPTION 3 : ASK FOR TIME

> *'I'm sorry, this has really taken me by surprise. I'd like to have some time to think about what you've said and then we can talk again.'*

This response is appropriate when the criticism has come as a shock or when, even after going through the first three stages, you are still feeling a strong temptation to slip into a fight or flight response.

GIVING UNWELCOME MESSAGES

HOW TO TELL PEOPLE WHAT THEY DON'T WANT TO HEAR

The reason that some conversations are difficult is that we have to tell the other person something that they don't want to hear – be it bad news, or a request that they change their behaviour. This chapter shows you how to:

- Give bad news, and manage the other person's expectations beforehand

- Tell someone that they need to change their behaviour

- Avoid playing the blame game

- Handle a strong emotional response from the other person

GIVING BAD NEWS

Part of the difficulty in breaking bad news is that it makes us feel uncomfortable. Some people cope with their discomfort by being too blunt *('you aren't ready for promotion')*, others by sugaring the pill so much that they give the other person a mixed message *('you have lots of potential')*.

 Revisit the pointers from chapter one about getting in the right mindset and deciding on the kind of style that you want to adopt in the conversation. Are you going to be sympathetic or matter of fact?

As with other types of difficult conversation, being well prepared is important. There will be four stages to the conversation:

 The start

 Letting the other person respond

 Giving the bad news

 Ending the conversation

GIVING UNWELCOME MESSAGES

GIVING BAD NEWS

Stage 1: Start the conversation

Ease into the conversation gently. Say something like, *'I'm afraid I have some bad news for you'* or *'I've been thinking about your intention to apply for a more senior role, and I have some reservations which I want to discuss with you'*.

Stage 2: Give the bad news

Move on to give them the bad news directly but tactfully: *'I don't think that you are ready for a promotion'*.

Stage 3: Let the other person respond

If they are angry or upset, let them express their emotions. Your aim here is to show empathy with how the other person is feeling. Try to avoid clichés such as *'I know how you feel'*, which can sound like token, rather than real, empathy. Phrases such as: *'I can understand this is disappointing for you'*, or *'I understand that this is unwelcome news'* demonstrate more genuine concern.

GIVING BAD NEWS

Stage 4: End the conversation

When you are preparing for the conversation, think about how you want to end the interaction. **For some types of bad news there may be further information that needs to be considered** – for example if you are making someone redundant, there will be practical arrangements to be discussed. It is often best to give this information in written form (the other person may not be able to take it in if you start bombarding them with facts when they are still feeling upset at the bad news). Alternatively, you can arrange to meet with them again to talk through any practical implications.

If there are no practicalities to be discussed, you can end the conversation when it feels diplomatic to do so.

Top Tip
It is often better to conduct the conversation at a neutral venue, or the other person's office so that you can take your leave when it feels appropriate.

MANAGING EXPECTATIONS

SETTING THE RIGHT LEVEL

Part of the art of telling people things that they don't want to hear is managing their expectations beforehand. Some of us are prone to raising expectations to a level that we can't always meet: we over-promise and under-deliver.

Imagine that your manager is giving you a new project. As he or she explains the task, you start to suspect that you might not be able to complete the work within the allotted time. At this point you can manage your manager's expectations by either:

Setting their expectations at the right level:
'I'll do my best to complete this on time, but I think it might over-run.'

or

Deliberately setting their expectations at a lower level:
'I won't be able to meet that deadline. Can we discuss extending it?'

MANAGING EXPECTATIONS
LOWERING EXPECTATIONS

The **benefits** of setting the other person's expectations at a lower level include:

- It reduces the likelihood of them being disappointed if/when the project over-runs, and makes the ensuing discussion less difficult

- There is more chance of them being pleasantly surprised if you manage to complete the project early or on time

The **disadvantage** is that you can be seen as negative, and a 'blocker' if you do it too often.

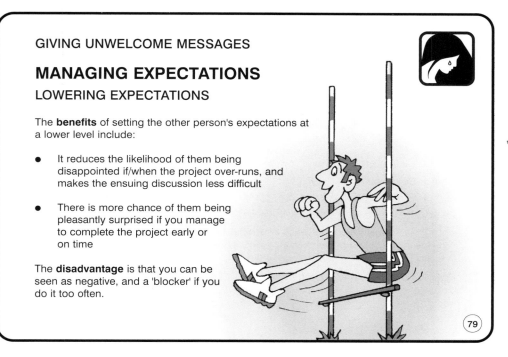

GIVING UNWELCOME MESSAGES

ASKING SOMEONE TO CHANGE
THEIR BEHAVIOUR
THE **SID** PROCESS

Imagine that your manager often gives you urgent work to do just before you are due to go home, which results in you working late.

Step 1: Be **S**pecific
Talk about the precise behaviour that is causing you a problem:

'When you give me urgent work to do just before I am due to leave....'

Step 2: Talk about the practical or emotional **I**mpact
'....it means that I either rush to do the work before I leave (and risk making mistakes) or I am late leaving, which means I miss my bus.'

Step 3: Say what your **D**esired outcome is
'It would really help me if we could have a quick chat half an hour before I leave, so I can see if there's anything you want me to do before I go.'

ASKING SOMEONE TO CHANGE THEIR BEHAVIOUR

AVOIDING INFLAMMATORY WORDS

'You should' *'You must'*	This is like wagging a finger in the other person's face. It sounds bossy and is likely to provoke either a parent or child response.
'Your problem is' *'Your attitude is'*	Both these phrases are provocative. Talking about the other person's attitude is risky because he or she has more insight into his or her attitude than you do – you are speculating. It's better to confine yourself to **talking about what the other person has actually done, or not done.**
'Your behaviour'	This can sound like a teacher talking to a schoolchild, and is likely to irritate the other person.
'You always' *'You never'*	These statements often produce the response along the lines of '*I don't **always**',* which then leads to an unhelpful dispute about the frequency of the behaviour that you want the other person to change.

AVOID PLAYING THE BLAME GAME

We play the blame game when our focus is on identifying who is at fault, rather than looking for ways of resolving the problem. The blame game starts when people are feeling defensive about something that has gone wrong. Here's how to avoid it:

- **State clearly at the start that you aren't interested in blaming anyone.**
  You simply want to explore what went wrong, and why

- **Be scrupulous about avoiding inflammatory phrases** like, *'you should have'* and *'your fault'*. Instead, ask *'what happened next?'* and *'how did that come about?'*

- **Be tactful but thorough** – get to the root of the problem but without accusing anyone

Focus on the future – use questions like, *'what should we do differently next time?'* and, *'what have we learned from this?'*

COPING WITH TEARS

GENUINE TEARS

If the other person is genuinely upset, perhaps tearful, you can respond by:

- **Stopping the conversation.** Don't try and carry on when the other person is in danger of being overwhelmed by emotion. They won't be able to think rationally

- **Asking *'do you want to take a moment?'*** Allow them time to compose themselves before continuing with the conversation

- **Empathising:** *'I can understand that this is distressing for you'*

- **Asking if they are able to carry on with the conversation.** If not, suggest that you take a ten minute break – perhaps put the kettle on – or, if they are very distressed, it might be better to postpone the conversation for a day or so

GIVING UNWELCOME MESSAGES

COPING WITH TEARS

CROCODILE TEARS

Occasionally you may find yourself dealing with someone who dissolves into tears **whenever there is the prospect of them being challenged about their performance or actions.** The underlying message is, *'I'm so fragile. Only a cruel and heartless person would upset me'.* Sometimes your intuition will tell you that the other person is behaving in a manipulative way.

If you suspect that this is the case, you can follow the same approach as with genuine tears, but **in a more matter of fact and less empathic way.** So you might say something like:

'I'm sorry that you seem to be upset by this. Do you want to take a moment before we carry on with the conversation?'

COPING WITH TANTRUMS

TURNING DOWN THE EMOTIONAL TEMPERATURE

First, and most importantly: **if the other person becomes violent or abusive, get out of the situation quickly.**

You can reduce the chances of an angry response by:

- **Avoiding strong eye contact.** When we stare into another person's eyes we activate more instinctive parts of the brain. In an intimate encounter this can heighten feelings of attraction, however in a conflict situation it can exacerbate angry feelings

- **Standing or sitting at right-angles to the other person.** Confronting someone face-to-face gives a 'me against you' message. Positioning yourself at a ninety degree angle enables you both to look in the same direction, creating a sense of 'we are trying to solve a problem together'

- **Gently mirroring the other person,** as described in chapter three

COPING WITH TANTRUMS
ALLOW THEM TO LET OFF STEAM

If the other person is full of angry feelings, they won't be able to listen and take in much of what you are saying, **so allow them a little time to express their emotions before trying to have a rational discussion.** If you are feeling uncomfortable, it can be tempting to try and 'put the lid' on their anger, but sit tight and wait for them to calm down a little before moving the conversation forward.

If, after a minute or so, the other person shows no signs of calming down, suggest that you both take a ten minute break before resuming the conversation.

SAY NO & MEAN IT

SAY NO & MEAN IT

WHY IT'S IMPORTANT

Being able to say 'no' is important if you are going to get what you want out of life and avoid being taken advantage of by others. Situations where you might need to give a clear 'no' include:

● Someone requesting that you take on extra work that you don't want to do

● Being asked to take responsibility for a project or task that you don't feel you have been trained to undertake

● When you feel pressurised or manipulated to do something that goes against your values

This chapter will help you to deal with the discomfort that you might feel around saying 'no,' and find practical ways of getting your message across.

SAY NO & MEAN IT

WHAT'S THE PROBLEM WITH SAYING 'NO'?

For some people, 'no' feels like the most difficult word in the English language.

Getting better at giving a confident and clear 'no' requires that you:

- Identify the head tapes that may be preventing you from saying 'no', or making you feel bad when you do

- Learn how to say 'no' in a way that reduces the other person's disappointment, and limits the damage to the relationship

- Develop ways of dealing with someone who won't accept your 'no' and tries to manipulate you

Nnnnyes!

HEAD TAPES

The first chapter of this book described how head tapes can prevent you from dealing effectively with difficult situations. Head tapes which can undermine your ability to say 'no' with conviction include:

> *'I must always be helpful.'*

> *'It is important to put others first.'*

If you feel guilty at the prospect of turning someone down, you might need to replace an existing head tape with a healthier one, eg:

> *'It's OK to say no.'*

> *'If I don't learn to say no, I'll burn myself out – then I won't be able to help anyone.'*

SAY NO & MEAN IT

DIFFERENT TYPES OF 'NO'
EMPATHIC & PRE-EMPTIVE

The empathic 'no'
You can soften your refusal by empathising with the other person:

'I'm sorry that I can't help you – I can see that you're in a bit of a fix, and I hope you manage to find someone who is able to help you out.'

Saying 'no' can count as a withdrawal from the emotional bank account – see chapter two. Empathising reduces the withdrawal.

The pre-emptive 'no'
The pre-emptive 'no' saves you from having to say 'no' at all.

Imagine you have heard that your manager is looking for someone to work overtime – something you don't want to do. Here you could use the pre-emptive 'no' by mentioning casually to your manager how many commitments you have outside of work at the moment – making it less likely that he or she will ask you to work the extra hours.

SAY NO & MEAN IT

DIFFERENT TYPES OF 'NO'

THE BROKEN RECORD

This technique can be useful when the other person doesn't want to accept your 'no', and tries to manipulate you. As the title suggests, it consists of restating your refusal in a short and simple manner. Eg:

Sam	*'I'm really busy – would you go to this afternoon's meeting in my place and take the minutes?'*
Pat	*'Sorry, Sam, but I'm very busy myself. **I won't be able to cover for you this afternoon.***'*
Sam	*'But I'm totally overwhelmed with work. I need some help.'*
Pat	*'I'm sorry to hear that. It sounds tough. Unfortunately **I won't be able to cover for you this afternoon.***'*
Sam	*'You're normally so helpful – why are letting me down now?'*
Pat	*'I'm glad you find me helpful, and I'm sorry you feel let down, but **I won't be able to cover for you this afternoon.***'*

EXPRESSING STRONG FEELINGS

WHEN & HOW TO EXPRESS YOUR FEELINGS

This chapter will help you to tackle a difficult conversation when **your** feelings are running high, for example when you feel someone has let you down. It shows you how to:

- Prepare yourself so as to maximise the chances of a positive outcome

- Pinpoint exactly what you are feeling, and what is triggering those emotions

- Talk about feelings in a way that does not provoke defensiveness in the other person

EXPRESSING STRONG FEELINGS

WHEN TO TALK ABOUT FEELINGS

You might be wondering if it is OK to talk about feelings in a business setting. Some workplaces have a rather macho culture where people are expected to get the job done, without any mention of feelings.

The truth is that everyone brings their feelings to work, and the most effective organisations and managers are those that recognise that workers are human beings with hopes, fears and preferences.

EXPRESSING STRONG FEELINGS

PREPARING FOR THE CONVERSATION

HAVE A CLEAR OBJECTIVE

A common mistake is to enter the conversation with the aim of *'getting things off my chest'*. This can lead to a relatively uncontrolled expression of emotion that merely exacerbates the difficulty between the two parties.

When preparing, it is vital that you identify a clear objective that sets out exactly what you want to achieve from the conversation. This is for yourself, not to be shared with the other party. For example:

'To tell Monica how let down I felt, so that she doesn't do it again.'

'To let Greg know how angry I felt about the way he talked to me.'

It is best if your objective is future oriented, **focused on how you want things to be from now on,** rather than going over past hurts or injustices.

EXPRESSING STRONG FEELINGS

PREPARING FOR THE CONVERSATION

SEE THE OTHER PERSON'S PERSPECTIVE

Preparing for a conversation where you express your feelings includes **imagining how things look from the other person's view.** If someone has hurt or angered you it is easy to fall into the trap of only seeing their bad qualities, or attributing negative motives to them.

If you see the other person in an unrealistically negative light it makes you more likely to adopt an accusing tone when you meet, which will only increase their defensiveness.

Here are some questions to ask yourself, which will help you see the other person's perspective:

'How can I see their intentions as positive?'

'How do I appear from their perspective?'

'What might they be afraid of, or anxious about?'

CLARIFYING YOUR OWN FEELINGS

Feelings can be complicated. Sometimes there is a mix of anger, disappointment, sadness and anxiety all rolled up into a ball of unhappiness about a particular situation. **Some of the feelings may have very little to do with the other person:** they are old feelings from earlier years (sometimes way back in childhood) which have been triggered again.

So, before embarking on a difficult conversation where you intend to talk about your feelings, you need to:

- Identify exactly what you are feeling

- Analyse what is causing the feeling

- Pinpoint the other person's role in contributing to your feelings

CLARIFYING YOUR OWN FEELINGS

'WHAT EXACTLY AM I FEELING?'

Try this: think about a situation that you find uncomfortable, or a person that you dislike. Have a look at the following list of emotions and see if you can identify the ones that are part of your uncomfortable feeling:

fear

regret

misery

sadness

disappointment

anxiety

impatience

anger

embarrassment

shame

rage

CLARIFYING YOUR OWN FEELINGS

'WHY AM I FEELING THIS WAY?'

Once you have identified exactly what you are feeling, the next step is to **work out specifically what is causing the feeling.** Often it is not just the other person's actions, but the underlying message contained in those actions that provokes our intense reaction. For example, if your manager repeatedly expects you to work late at short notice, the underlying message might be interpreted as:

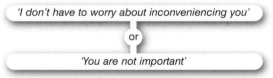

'I don't have to worry about inconveniencing you'

or

'You are not important'

Identifying what you perceive as the underlying message can help to explain why you are having such a strong reaction to what appears to be, in this example, a relatively common workplace irritation.

CLARIFYING YOUR OWN FEELINGS

'WHO IS RESPONSIBLE FOR ME FEELING THIS WAY?'

Our interpretation of another person's actions, and the feelings this generates, **are both influenced by our personal history.**

Example

If someone had the sense when young that their parents did not value them, he or she might grow up sensitised to any suggestion that another person does not value them.

Sometimes our sensitivity is set too high – we interpret someone else's thoughtlessness as them actively discounting our worth. This can lead us to act in a way that looks like an over-reaction, from the other person's perspective.

CLARIFYING YOUR OWN FEELINGS
'HOW MUCH OF THIS IS ABOUT THE OTHER PERSON?'

Once you have thought about your personal history and the particular sensitivities that it has left you with, you can clarify the extent to which your feelings are caused by the other person's action.

You might decide that your manager's expectations are annoying, but the reason you are so angry is that their behaviour has triggered your sensitivity to feeling taken-for-granted. This recognition can help you to keep their behaviour in perspective. You might decide that:

20% of your anger is because you don't like working late.

40% is because you feel your manager often takes you for granted.

40% of it is provoked by your childhood memories being triggered.

So, instead of saying, *'I'm sick of you expecting me to work late at short notice'* you can say, *'I find it difficult when you ask me to work late at short notice because often it's not convenient for me'*.

STAY IN YOUR OWN BUSINESS

One of the principles of conducting a difficult conversation is to make sure that you stay in your own business. This means talking about your own feelings, and the way that the other person's behaviour affects those feelings, but **not getting into speculation about their attitude or intention.**

If you restrict yourself to talking about what the other person has done, or not done, you are on much firmer ground than if you enter into a debate about what their feelings or intentions might be – for the simple reason that they are the expert on their thoughts and feelings, whereas you are just speculating based on the actions that you have witnessed.

Don't engage their primitive brain
Remember to use the tips earlier in the book on standing or sitting at right-angles, and avoiding too much strong eye contact.

EXPRESSING STRONG FEELINGS

TALK ABOUT, DON'T 'ACT OUT'!

Experienced negotiators **talk about** their feelings rather than **acting them out** (acting out their feelings might involve banging the table, or walking out of the negotiation). This approach of naming your feelings but not acting them out can work well in a range of situations. For example:

Instead of glaring at the other person and talking more loudly, you might say calmly but clearly, *'I feel angry at the way you have undermined me.'*

If you feel the other person is trying to manipulate you or 'pull a fast one' you might be tempted to fire a series of questions at them to try and catch them out. This is likely to provoke a defensive response – a better approach would be to say, *'I'm feeling confused and a little worried about your suggestion. Could you clarify it'.*

TEN TIPS TO TAKE AWAY

TEN TIPS TO TAKE AWAY

1. Think through your mindset, replacing unhelpful head tapes.

2. Prepare thoroughly, including clarifying your objective.

3. Identify the unconscious factors such as fight/flight and parent/child dynamics that may influence the conversation.

4. Take time to create the right atmosphere at the start of the conversation.

5. Use body language, deliberate questions and tailored language to make an impact.

TEN TIPS TO TAKE AWAY

6. Remember that you have the right to say 'no'. Use broken record, empathy and the pre-emptive 'no' to get your message across.

7. Avoid the blame game – keep your difficult conversations 'future-focused'.

8. Give bad news tactfully but clearly.

9. Don't be put off if the other person expresses strong feelings.

10. Examine your own feelings, and identify what is about you and what is about the other person.

FURTHER INFORMATION

READING LIST

Influence Science & Practice,
Robert Cialdini, Allyn & Bacon, 2001

Influencing with Integrity: Management Skills for Communication and Negotiation,
Genie Z. Laborde, Crown House

Words that Change Minds: Mastering the Language of Influence,
Shelle Rose Charvet, Kendall/Hunt, 1997

Assertiveness at Work: A Practical Guide to Handling Awkward Situations,
Ken Back and Kate Back,
McGraw-Hill, 2005

Working It Out At Work,
Julie Hay, Sherwood, 1993

Improve Your People Skills,
Peter Honey, Chartered Institute of Personnel & Development, 2001

The Seven Habits of Highly Effective People,
Stephen R. Covey,
Simon & Schuster, 2004

About the Author

Peter English
Peter English has over sixteen years experience of helping thousands of managers and professionals to develop their interpersonal effectiveness. He has a particular interest in helping people at all organisational levels become more assertive and confident in tackling difficult conversations.

Contact
Peter can be contacted by email at pete@peterenglish.co.uk

This pocketbook also by Peter English

Pocketbooks – *available in both paperback and digital formats*

360 Degree Feedback
Absence Management
Appraisals
Assertiveness
Balance Sheet
Body Language
Business Planning
Career Transition
Coaching
Cognitive Behavioural Coaching
Communicator's
Competencies
Creative Manager's
C.R.M.
Cross-cultural Business
Customer Service
Decision-making
Delegation
Developing People
Discipline & Grievance
Diversity
Emotional Intelligence
Employment Law
Empowerment
Energy and Well-being
Facilitator's
Feedback
Flexible Workplace

Handling Complaints
Handling Resistance
Icebreakers
Impact & Presence
Improving Efficiency
Improving Profitability
Induction
Influencing
International Trade
Interviewer's
I.T. Trainer's
Key Account Manager's
Leadership
Learner's
Management Models
Manager's
Managing Assessment Centres
Managing Budgets
Managing Cashflow
Managing Change
Managing Customer Service
Managing Difficult Participants
Managing Recruitment
Managing Upwards
Managing Your Appraisal
Marketing
Meetings
Memory

Mentoring
Motivation
Negotiator's
Networking
NLP
Nurturing Innovation
Openers & Closers
People Manager's
Performance Management
Personal Success
Positive Mental Attitude
Presentations
Problem Behaviour
Problem Solving
Project Management
Psychometric Testing
Resolving Conflict
Reward
Sales Excellence
Salesperson's
Self-managed Development
Starting In Management
Storytelling
Strategy
Stress
Succeeding at Interviews
Tackling Difficult Conversations
Talent Management

Teambuilding Activities
Teamworking
Telephone Skills
Telesales
Thinker's
Time Management
Trainer's
Training Evaluation
Training Needs Analysis
Transfer of Learning
Virtual Teams
Vocal Skills
Working Relationships
Workplace Politics
Writing Skills

Pocketfiles

Trainer's Blue Pocketfile of
Ready-to-use Activities

Trainer's Green Pocketfile of
Ready-to-use Activities

Trainer's Red Pocketfile of
Ready-to-use Activities

28.03.13

ORDER FORM

	No. copies

Your details

Name _____

Position _____

Company _____

Address _____

_____

_____

Telephone _____

Fax _____

E-mail _____

VAT No. (EC companies) _____

Your Order Ref _____

Please send me:

The <u>Tackling Difficult Conversations</u> Pocketbook ☐

The _____ Pocketbook ☐

The _____ Pocketbook ☐

The _____ Pocketbook ☐

Order by Post
MANAGEMENT POCKETBOOKS LTD
LAUREL HOUSE, STATION APPROACH,
ALRESFORD, HAMPSHIRE SO24 9JH UK

Order by Phone, Fax or Internet
Telephone: +44 (0)1962 735573
Facsimile: +44 (0)1962 733637
Email: sales@pocketbook.co.uk
Web: www.pocketbook.co.uk

Customers in USA should contact:
Management Pocketbooks
2427 Bond Street, University Park, IL 60466
Telephone: 866 620 6944 Facsimile: 708 534 7803
Email: mp.orders@ware-pak.com
Web: www.managementpocketbooks.com

MANAGEMENT POCKETBOOKS